BOURNEMOUTH
IN OLD PHOTOGRAPHS

BOURNEMOUTH SQUARE in 1870

BOURNEMOUTH
IN OLD PHOTOGRAPHS

COLLECTED BY
MICHAEL COLMAN

ALAN SUTTON
1989

Alan Sutton Publishing
Gloucester

First published 1989

British Library Cataloguing in Publication Data

Bournemouth in old photographs.
1. Dorset. Bournemouth, history.
I. Colman, Michael
942.338

ISBN 0-86299-706-7

Typesetting and origination by
Alan Sutton Publishing
Printed in Great Britain by
Dotesios Printers Limited

CONTENTS

THE TWO HORSE OMNIBUS from Richmond Hill to Winton in 1900. A third horse was often added to help pull the bus up hills.

INTRODUCTION

Bournemouth does not exist. The year is 1800: Britain is at war with France, and Napoleon is about to become emperor. Beethoven has written his first symphony, and William Pitt the Younger, as Prime Minister, is engaged with his reforms and with the French. Following the example of the Prince Regent, fashionable London society has for half a century been at Brighton, and after many visits George III has made Weymouth his summer home. Where Bournemouth now stands a wild, desolate heathland stretches from Poole to Christchurch, uninhabited save for a few fishing huts. There is not one inhabited house within three miles of today's Square.

Yet on this same spot, exactly 100 years later, stands a thriving health resort of 60,000 inhabitants which has become the second largest seaside resort in the United Kingdom, a rate of growth unparalleled by any other town in Britain.

Why this phenomenal mushrooming of the town from a wilderness? Every irregularity of the soil had been there since prehistoric times; in the words of Thomas Hardy, 'not a sod having been turned there since the time of the Caesars'. Even earlier, in Neolithic times, the megalithic monolith builders from the eastern Mediterranean had passed this way, and nearby Hengistbury Head had become an important settlement. Hengistbury was Britain's first port, carrying out friendly trade with the Romans, but it then faded into obscurity. It was not until 1407 that the Bourne stream is mentioned in records as 'La Bournemowthe'. The 'Fall of the Burn' is shown on a map of 1567, and 'Burnemouthe' on a map of 1575, showing how closely the name is derived from the Anglo-Saxon words 'Burna', a small stream, and 'mûth', a delta or mouth.

This was then the haunt of smugglers, who along with a few gypsies and fishermen had the place to themselves for centuries. On the maze of pathways that covered the heath, travellers were sometimes startled by the sight of up to 300 horsemen with a convoy of 20 or 30 waggons loaded with kegs of spirits, on their way to their hiding places in the New Forest. Brisk trade was done quite openly with the local gentry, particularly in French brandy.

In those days Elizabeth I was on the throne and the idea of seaside bathing would have been regarded with revulsion. At Cambridge, scholars who dared to bathe by day or night were set in the stocks and, upon a second offence, were whipped with rods. Another two centuries passed before doctors began to recommend sea bathing for invalids and seaside resorts such as Brighton and Weymouth came into being. Bournemouth even then was 'a desolate spot', a place of 'unreclaimed solitude' but, for Louis Tregonwell, its very seclusion and mild climate was its great attraction.

With the start of the Napoleonic Wars in 1796, Tregonwell, as Captain of the Dorset Yeomanry, became responsible for the defences of the area, which as early as 1575 had been noted by the Earl of Southampton as a place suitable for an enemy landing; 'We finde at Bournemouth within the west baye at Christchurche a place very easy For the ennemye to lande there conteyning by estimacion oon quarter of a myle in length, being voyde of all inhabiting'. Tregonwell began to make trips to the area with his wife, who became enamoured of the spot. In 1809 an inn was built, the first building in Bournemouth, and it was here they stayed in July 1810 while on holiday at Mudeford. Mrs Tregonwell had recently suffered the tragic loss of an infant son on its christening day and her husband readily agreed to her suggestion that they build a house there. They completed their mansion, surrounded by shrubberies and plantations, in 1812 and soon many society friends began to visit their new home. So begins the story of Bourne, as it came to be known. The Tregonwells embarked on a building programme to provide accommodation for family, friends and for letting. By 1826 houses were being advertised to rent, some with 'a bathing machine and a hot bath'. However, there were still only six houses in Bourne. By 1842 the land either side of the Bourne stream was owned by the Gervis and Tregonwell estates. The Gervis estate, to the east of the stream, consisted of the Westover Villas, the Bath Hotel and Belle Vue Boarding House, in all amounting to twenty houses. The Tregonwell side of the brook to the west contained some six houses, a total of less than thirty houses.

The coach road between Southampton and Poole had been made in 1810 and ran through Bourne bottom, near the present Town Hall. At this time the stream ran across the road more-or-less at will, the only dry crossing for pedestrians was by means of a plank laid across the stream, connecting the two estates at the present site of the Square. A brick bridge was built in 1849, and a new road was constructed to replace Tregonwell's earlier road which had become obliterated by sand. A few shops opened at the foot of Commercial Road in 1851, and now

Bourne could number its own resident surgeon among its growing population. However, it was still only a fishing community of 695 inhabitants; can it be possible that this figure could swell over the next 50 years to a staggering 60,000?

The image being presented to visitors at this stage had begun to cause concern: there was no drainage of any sort and cesspools had become a hazard. These and other problems led to the implementation of the 1856 Bournemouth Improvement Act, when Bournemouth became a town. It now had a sea frontage of two miles, and other communities were springing up in the vicinity. The telegraph reached here in 1860, at which time Westbourne contained six houses.

The idea of a jetty or landing stage had been discussed as early as 1847, but it was in 1855 that a retractable jetty on wheels was rather hurriedly built after rumours of a visit by the Queen. The first permanent pier was begun in 1860 by Mr David Thornbury, an engineer of some reputation, who boasted that it was a 'trifling occupation' to 'knock off a pier'. Made of timber, it was immediately swept away by stormy seas. A new pier finally opened in 1861, but repairs continually had to be made until one day in 1867 when a great gale struck, and stormy seas dumped the whole structure back onto the beach. It was again repaired, but further disasters followed and by 1877 it had been damaged beyond all use. A totally new pier was devised; the pier of today which was opened in 1880 by the Lord Mayor of London.

The railways had arrived at Christchurch in 1862, but Bournemouth did not have a station of its own until 1870. This was situated in what became the goods yard of the present station. Bournemouth Central, then known as Bournemouth East, opened in 1885 and soon thousands of visitors were arriving daily. Bournemouth West had opened in 1874 and on one day alone in August 1884 recorded the arrival of 6,500 trippers.

The first horse bus service had been introduced in 1872, running to Southbourne, and soon other routes were introduced, mainly from Christchurch to Poole. The first tram service ran from Poole to County Gates in 1901, but the line was not extended through Westbourne due to opposition from residents of Poole Road. Trams finally ran through Bournemouth Square in 1902, and soon the horse buses were rendered obsolete.

Happily, the start of this century coincided with the new popular hobby of photography, and millions of Kodak cameras were being sold around the world. Photography in Bournemouth started with the talented Robert Day, some of whose excellent pictures appear on the following pages. He worked from a small hut at the foot of Richmond Hill, in the days when location photography required carrying equipment of almost expeditionary proportions involving cameras, chemicals and even a portable dark-room tent.

It is almost 140 years since some of the scenes in this book were photographed, and in those years Bournemouth has changed dramatically from a village with the look of the Wild West. If its rate of growth continues, what will it look like in as many years again?

Finally, I hope that this book will bring back happy memories to many Bournemouth folk and recall a time long gone. There must be many fascinating photographs of Bournemouth lying forgotten in albums and attics. Perhaps one day these might appear in a second volume of the sights of old Bournemouth.

SECTION ONE

The Square

A CONVERSATION IN THE SQUARE in 1872. At this time the Gardens extended across the Square to the foot of Richmond Hill, where St Andrew's Scotch Church is here pictured in the year it was built.

IN EARLIER DAYS the Bourne stream ran over the road more-or-less unhindered; pedestrians crossed here by means of a plank laid across the brook. A brick bridge was built in 1849, and is pictured here c. 1866.

HACKNEY CARRIAGES wait by the Victoria Library in 1890, at a time when St Andrew's Presbyterian Church, on the left, was only two years old.

THE SCOTCH CHURCH at the foot of Richmond Hill replaced an earlier structure made from galvanized iron. It is pictured in 1867, when Richmond Hill was probably Bournemouth's busiest road.

THE WILTSHIRE AND DORSET BANK in the late 1860s, later taken over by Hankinson's estate agency.

THE VIEW FROM TERRACE MOUNT, looking towards Old Christchurch Road and Gervis Place. Southbourne Terrace, where W.H. Smith now stands, is pictured at the time of its original construction in 1863.

LOCAL LANDMARKS provide excellent clues when dating a photograph. The tower of St Peter's, on the right, was not completed until June 1871, and the Scotch Church in the centre was demolished in early 1872. In this way the date can be narrowed to within a few months.

PROFESSIONAL PHOTOGRAPHY IN BOURNEMOUTH began in the small shack visible to the right of the Scotch Church. This was the studio of Robert Day, who took some of the pictures in this book. This photograph was taken in 1875.

A PANORAMA OF BOURNEMOUTH in 1901. On the site of the Scotch Church stand the Central and Empress Hotels. Only 26 years separate this view from the one above.

'THE BRIDGE', as the Square was called when this picture was taken in 1868. Shops had begun to open at the foot of Commercial Road (far right) in 1851, when the population of Bournemouth numbered 695. On the far left is Victoria Villa, home of Mr Hankinson the estate agent, whose business lay adjacently.

SOUTHBOURNE TERRACE, the site of today's W.H. Smith. The gardens were little more than meadowland when this photograph was taken in 1868.

THE VIEW OVER BOURNEMOUTH in 1868. The Westover Villas stretch away to the right, these were fine detached residences built in the Italianate style. The small building on the corner, at the junction of Old Christchurch Road and Gervis Place, is the site of the first offices of Rebbeck's estate agent, later Dolcis for many years and now a branch of Saxone.

LOOKING DOWN RICHMOND HILL in around 1873, showing Exeter Road in the distance.

THE VIEW FROM OLD CHRISTCHURCH ROAD in around 1865, showing how one could then walk across the Square without meeting a soul!

A THREE HORSE DOUBLE-DECKER, carrying passengers neatly bedecked in boaters, climbs the Old Christchurch Road in 1901. On the left one can see how ladders were used to reach the top deck.

THE SQUARE in 1905.

THE TRAM TO BOSCOMBE passes what is today the National Westminster Bank. Trams came to Bournemouth in 1902, but in this picture of 1910 excursions in a horse carriage for 1s. are advertised.

A TRAM DESCENDS RICHMOND HILL in 1905. This line opened in 1903, and trams using the line had special brakes.

TRAMS, CARTS, CARRIAGES AND A BICYCLE make their way across the Square in this postcard view of around 1904.

A PEACEFUL SCENE in 1900. The Victorian lady in the foreground crosses the road at a leisurely pace. On the left are the sleek lines of a landau, no doubt waiting for the thousands of trippers arriving daily by rail.

PASSENGERS WITH PARASOLS and in boaters about to leave on a charabanc excursion in around 1914.

THE READING OF THE PROCLAMATION of the accession of King Edward VII on 25 January 1901.

THE SQUARE is first mentioned in records of 1858. In that year PC Smith was Bournemouth's only policeman. The force was increased to three in 1869.

THE TRAM SHELTER, which replaced the earlier roundabout. The white clock, known as the Norton clock, is still a landmark today.

TROLLEY BUSSES were introduced in 1936, and these familiar yellow vehicles with their maroon and green stripes did service until 1969, when overhead wires, used since the introduction of trams in 1902, finally became obsolete.

MOTOR BUSSES began to appear in 1964, which dates this picture as being sometime between 1964 and 1969. The white clock was placed on a pedestal in 1948. Behind it stands the old bus station which was destroyed by fire in 1974. Entrance was by means of the steep ramp seen at the front.

SECTION TWO
Pier and Sea Front

BATH CHAIRS AND DONKEY CARRIAGES wait outside the entrance to the pier in around 1910.

THE VIEW FROM THE PIER in around 1867, showing the Belle Vue Hotel and Sydenham's Reading Rooms. On the far left can be seen the remains of Bournemouth's first landing stage, the jetty of 1855.

THE PIER APPROACH in 1872. Sydenham's, with the sunblinds, is in the middle of the picture, and, on the right, the first Fancy Bazaar can be seen. Mr Sydenham sold 'Stationery of every description: new and fashionable music, soda-water, lemonade and ginger beer, tea and coffee'. There were also 'pianofortes for sale or hire'!

THE WOODEN PIER of 1861. Local landmarks again make the dating of this picture a simple affair. St Peter's tower, visible on the skyline above the shelter, was completed in 1871 and, by 1872, eight lamps had been placed on the pier. A date of early 1872 gives a margin of error of only a few months, accurate enough for a picture taken 117 years ago!

TAKING THE AIR on the wooden pier. Visitors to the pier in 1868 sometimes complained of the stench emanating from the toll-house. Subsequently it was discovered that the keeper, Mr Llewellyn, was a taxidermist. The practice was stopped forthwith!

THE PIERHEAD in 1860. This photograph shows the stacks of huge timbers waiting to be pile driven into the sand to make the wooden pier of 1861. On the extreme right the original baths can be seen.

THE PIER APPROACH in around 1870, when the pony and trap at the pier entrance seem almost surplus to requirements.

KEEPING A CLEAN IMAGE in the mid-1870s. In 1867 a great gale had unceremoniously dumped the entire pier back onto the beach. It was repaired, but was now 300 ft shorter. It was again wrecked in 1876 with wreckage found as far away as Swanage.

A VIEW OF BROOKSIDE, on the right, where the eminent preacher and poet John Keble lived until his death in 1865. The bridge crossed the Bourne at the entrance to the Lower Gardens. A comparison of these houses with those in the background of the above picture gives a very clear idea of where the bridge stood.

LET THERE BE LIGHT! Lamps were placed on the pier in 1872, providing an excellent subject for one intrepid photographer.

THE EAST BEACH in around 1900. Rows of bathing machines stretch along the shore, but very few of these holidaymakers seem to have got their feet wet. On the left is the Fancy Bazaar and on the skyline are the Bath Hotel and East Cliff Hall, later the Russell-Coates museum.

BOURNEMOUTH BEACH in 1865. The boy is standing on the remains of the 1855 Jetty.

Paddling at Bournemouth

A PADDLE BY THE PIER at around the turn of the century. The ramp was used as a landing stage for small boats. Could this be a regatta day?

NEW TECHNOLOGY MEETS THE OLD. The electric lift was constructed in 1908, the same year as a similar lift was installed on the West Cliff. In this picture of the East Cliff lift, an expensively attired attendant waits beside a bath chair.

THE WEST BEACH before the advent of the promenade.

ROWING BOATS on the west beach in the 1920s. A landing stage on wheels stands by the water's edge and on the skyline is the Highcliff Hotel where the future King Edward VII stayed in 1900.

A PANORAMIC VIEW of the pier c. 1901. Have these promenaders just been listening to the military band in the bandstand, or have they been enjoying themselves on the roller skating deck?

View from Pier Shelter, Bournemouth.

A PROMENADE ON THE PIER. Construction of the present pier began in 1878 after a series of disasters with the old wooden pier. It was opened on 11 April 1880 by the Lord Mayor of London. This view dates from around 1903.

The Sands from Pier, W. Bournemouth.

481

ROWING BOATS must have been popular, but this photograph is unusual in that it shows a boat actually on the sea, if only just!

A SPRIG OF LEAVES behind the lady in the foreground is held coyly away from the sight of the sedate ladies and gentlemen seated on the pier. A gift from an admirer? Meanwhile, the little girl on the right gives a big smile for the camera.

BATHING MACHINES were not allowed within 200 yards of the pier when they were first introduced. The men's machines were in the foreground while the ladies' were nearer the pier.

THE ZIG ZAG PATH was fun for a child on a scooter, as the author once found out with disastrous results!

THE PIER APPROACH. On the left is the old entrance hall and in the centre is the Bournemouth Club by the new Promenade.

THE PERAMBULATOR on the left can have no brakes as the lady is holding it behind her on her way down the West Cliff in around 1903.

THE READING OF THE CHARTER OF INCORPORATION on 27 August 1890 at 3.20 p.m. It was evidently a rainy afternoon.

THE EAST CLIFF after the building of the first section of the Undercliff Drive, opened in 1907.

THE UNDERCLIFF DRIVE had been discussed as early as 1878. On the day that it opened in November 1907 Mr Russell Coates gave his collection of art treasures to the town, to be housed in the East Cliff Hall, which was given to the town on the same day by his wife. The hall had been a birthday present from her husband.

THE FLIGHT INTO EGYPT. The sand modeller used to work on the western corner of the promenade by the pier. Only sand, water and colour were used.

DARK SUITS AND DARK CARS make up this uncomfortably crowded scene on the Undercliff Drive in the early 1930s, when an eight mile per hour limit was in force. Car enthusiasts might spot the Morris Major, the Austin 12 and three 1933 Austin Ruby's.

A PARADE OF VINTAGE CARS on the sea front in the early 1930s. By the pier are the Skylark boats, prompting the cry 'Any more for the Skylark?'

SECTION THREE

Town Centre

THE CENTRE OF THE TOWN in 1860, showing the junction of Old Christchurch Road and Gervis Place. Across the entrance to what is now Post Office Road stands the Tregonwell Arms, built by Sir George Ivision Tapps in 1809. This was the first building in Bournemouth.

THE TREGONWELL ARMS. It was here that the Tregonwells stayed on one of their visits to Bournemouth, deciding them to build a house of their own in this place of 'unreclaimed solitude'.

THE BATH HOTEL as it was in 1846. Built by Sir George Gervis in 1838, it was later purchased and enlarged by Mr Russell Coates. In later years it was much frequented by royalty.

PORTMAN LODGE was one of the earliest houses in Bournemouth. It was originally built by Mr Tregonwell for his butler, Symes, but was later used for letting and as family accommodation.

TREGONWELL'S MANSION of 1812, the first house in Bournemouth, later became Newlyn's Hotel and was subsequently taken over by the Marchioness of Exeter in 1820, giving Exeter Road its name. The centre part of the building is still preserved as part of the Royal Exeter Hotel.

LOOKING TOWARDS TERRACE COTTAGE, near Exeter Road, in 1865. The cottage was used by the Tregonwells as family accommodation; the site later became the Hotel Melville.

SHELLEY'S HEART lies here in St Peter's churchyard – or so it is said. Percy Bysshe Shelley was drowned off the coast of Italy on 8 July 1822. When the body reappeared, identifiable only by the volumes of poetry in the coat pockets, it was buried in the sand and cremated on the beach a month later to allow burial in the Protestant Cemetary in Rome. The heart, which apparently would not burn, was 'snatched from the flames' by his friend, author Edward Trelawny, and was eventually to come into the possession of Shelley's widow. In 1883 the poet's daughter-in-law, Lady Shelley, told how the relic, 'having become shrunk and withered', had been placed by Shelley's widow 'in a little silken bag, and slipped between the pages of *Adonais*, in that part of the poem which deals with immortality'. Shelley's ashes were removed from Rome and placed in the tomb of his son Percy Florence Shelley upon his death in 1889, and it is possible that the heart or whatever relic it was that existed was placed secretly in the tomb by the Revd M.W.F. St. John, Canon of Gloucester and Lady Shelley's nephew. Shelley's widow, Mary Wollstonecraft Shelley, was the author of *Frankenstein*, written while she was just 21 years old.

ST PETER'S in 1879, the year the spire was added. The statues near the pinnacles at the base of the spire were originally intended for the porch of Bristol Cathedral. On the left is Church House, later the site of Beales.

A LATER VIEW OF ST PETER'S in the 1920s, with what appears to be a Rolls Royce parked in Gervis Place outside what was later Minns Music shop.

THE VIEW FROM TERRACE MOUNT, 1875. St Peter's is spireless and the Pleasure Gardens are in an early stage of formation, having been enclosed only a few years previously.

THE RUSTIC BRIDGE in 1863. This toll-bridge was built by Thomas Settle in 1853 and linked Gervis Place with Old Christchurch Road. It spanned a glen called Church Glen and stood exactly on the spot today occupied by Bournemouth Arcade. The toll charged was $\frac{1}{2}d$.

RAPIDLY EXPANDING BOURNEMOUTH. In 1894 Bournemouth had eight churches, four banks, three newspapers and a population of 37,650. Seven years later, when this view of the Square was taken, the population had increased to nearly 60,000.

EXETER ROAD, looking towards the pier. On the right stands a milk cart in the days when one brought one's own jug and had it filled.

LOOKING DOWN RICHMOND HILL in 1880. The local milkman poses for the camera.

BOURNEMOUTH ARCADE (the Gervis Arcade) and Bright's Stores in 1900. *Bright's Guide to Bournemouth* says that 'During the winter season the Arcade is the favourite promenade of the town; and without doubt one of the most interesting sights to be observed in Bournemouth is the motley concourse of fashion and beauty which will be found in the Arcade on a wet or dull day'.

THE SQUARE AND UPPER GARDENS from the Mont Dore in around 1899.

THE TOWN CENTRE c. 1900. On the left stands the Mont Dore, now the Town Hall, which was fitted with every conceivable luxury. The ground floor alone consisted of dining rooms, tennis-court, skating-rink, winter gardens and several other rooms. It offered the famous Mont Dore cure, comprising of vapour, needle and douche, baths, inhalation halls for vapour and spray and, ominously, 'arrangements for throat and nasal irrigation'. The telephone number was Bournemouth 3.

The Gardens

PUSHING THE BABY through the almost deserted Gardens in the 1890s.

THE UPPER GARDENS looking towards Commercial Road: half an acre of these gardens were later used to enlarge the Square.

THE VALLEY OF THE BOURNE was described in 1846 as 'one long, marshy, rushy hollow'.

War Memorial &Town Hall, Bournemouth. 217.

THE TOWN HALL was established in the old Mont Dore in 1921. The War Memorial was unveiled a year later.

The Upper Gardens, Bournemouth.

WHEN BOURNEMOUTH BEGAN the Bourne was a trout stream, and a decoy pond stood on the site of today's Upper Gardens. It was called Decoy Pond Meadow until 1851.

TWO VIEWS OF THE IRON BRIDGE across the Bourne in around 1900. St Andrew's Presbyterian Church, next to the site of today's Fortes, suffered damage during the Second World War when the spire became unsafe and had to be removed.

THE FOUNTAIN C. 1905. Already examples of 'carpet bedding' appear around its base.

THE SAME SCENE in later years.

FOOTPATHS were made either side of the Bourne brook in 1869. In 1870, two seats were placed in the Pleasure Gardens. This view dates from around 1908.

COMING BACK FROM THE BEACH. This shows the entrance to the Gardens at the start of the century, a view which has changed very little over the years.

A PLETHORA OF PALM TREES at the entrance to the Central Gardens.

A WALK IN THE GARDENS. No other seaside resort can boast such a large area of pleasure gardens, parks and open spaces.

THE INVALIDS' WALK in around 1900. Bournemouth was once known as a place of recuperation for invalids, but after the First World War this rather unfortunate name was changed to The Pine Walk.

45 BOURNEMOUTH. — The Invalids Walk. — LL.

PROMENADERS IN THE INVALIDS' WALK at the turn of the century.

THE RUSTIC BANDSTAND on the left was the forerunner of today's bandstand. Concerts were given by a military band made up from members of the Municipal Orchestra.

THE PINE WALK in around 1925.

The Children's Corner, Bournemouth.

CHILDRENS' CORNER in the Pleasure Gardens, looking in 1930 much as it does today.

CHILDREN'S CORNER BOURNEMOUTH.

THE SLIGHT CURRENT of the Bourne was ideal for sailing one's boat; the children on the right seem absorbed by theirs. Evidently a stick came in very handy for prodding one's boat when it got stuck!

HATS AND PARASOLS — positively fearful of the sun.

FROM THE TOP OF THE GARDENS one could sail one's boat almost to the Pier Approach; these children are busy with theirs in around 1925.

THE GARDENS in the 1930s. The new Pavilion can be seen on the skyline.

THE FOUNTAIN in the Upper Gardens.

SECTION FIVE

Westbourne

WESTBOURNE contained only some half-dozen houses in the 1860s and, from Poole Hill to Alum Chine, there was only open heathland. This picture shows Westbourne during the snows of 1881. It was taken by chemist Mr G.W. Taylor, whose shop is behind the figure with the shovel. On the left is J. Batt's Fancy Bazaar and Library, and next door carcasses hang in the window of Wareham's Butchers. To the right of Taylor's a tricycle is parked outside Hayter's, the coal merchants.

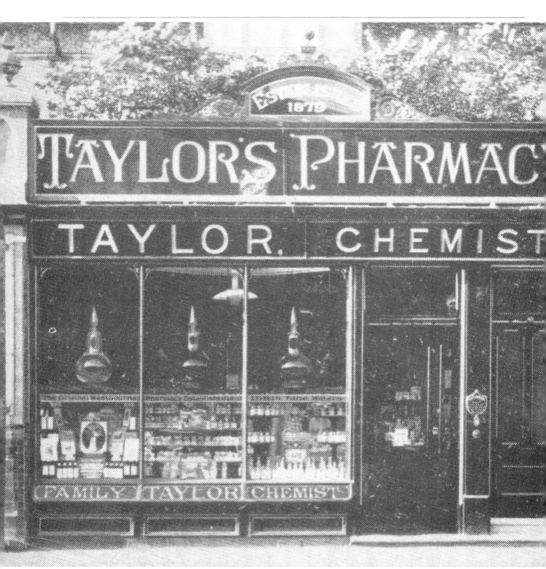

MR TAYLOR was a keen amateur photographer and took this photograph of his shop. The three coloured carboys in the window were a familiar sight for many years.

POOLE ROAD LOOKING EASTWARDS, taken from above Taylor's. The fine houses opposite had stood for a mere ten years or so when they were demolished to make way for the row of shops still found there today.

POOLE ROAD, NORTH SIDE, looking westwards, photographed from a point approximately opposite Pine Tree Glen.

The County Gates and Branksome Avenue.

COUNTY GATES AND BRANKSOME AVENUE *c.* 1906. There never was a gate that separated Hampshire and Dorset here. In 1818 the boundary had been moved from Durley Chine to Alum Chine and it was purely coincidental that the border fell across the gates to the lodge of Branksome Tower, which had been built in 1835 by Charles Packe MP.

OPPOSITE COUNTY GATES, at Hatfield, lived Dr Matthews, pictured here in 1926 with members of his family and brand new Essex.

THE EARLY 1950s: parked on the left is a 2.4 litre Riley and, on the right, stands the lamp with the red top which was a landmark for many years.

THE PNEU SCHOOL in Alumhurst Road, pictured while it was still a private house.

'THE GREEK DANCE' — an episode in the Parents' Day programme at the PNEU on Wednesday, 20 July 1932.

THE PNEU SCHOOL (not the PNEU pictured opposite) stood at the corner of Groveley Road and Alumhurst Road. On the far right of the group stands Marjorie Johnson, who at the age of 18 wrote a remarkable and historically important book on the life of Napoleon which was published in London, New York and Toronto. Her sister Myrtle was the best selling authoress of the dramatic novel *Hanging Johnny*, written when she too was only 18 years of age. Efforts have recently been made to discover the whereabouts of the Johnson sisters; does anyone know?

TRAMCAR NO. 52 to Boscombe takes on passengers by the Westbourne Congregational Church in around 1907. A tram-line was extended from Poole to County Gates in 1901 but due to opposition from the residents of Poole Road, a tramline through Westbourne was delayed until 1902. Just visible on the right is the drum clock which stood outside the shop of Mr Charles Dale, the borough meteorologist.

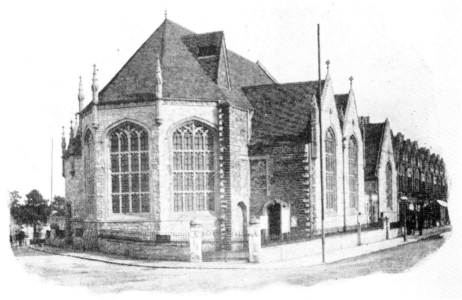

THE CONGREGATIONAL CHURCH which stood opposite County Gates was built in 1897 and is pictured here in 1900. It was later demolished to make way for a roundabout.

WESTBOURNE in 1909, looking westwards. The Arcade is on the left, and tramcar No. 14 to Christchurch passes Landseer Road on the right.

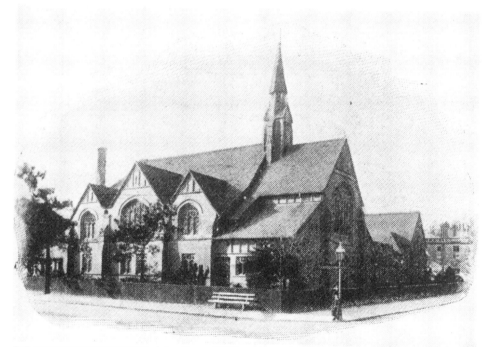

THE WEST CLIFF TABERNACLE dates from 1890 and stands at the junction of Grosvenor Road and Poole Road, seen here in 1901.

OPPOSITE WEST STATION was Isaac and Co., Malmesbury Dairies, pictured here c. 1901. Outside stands their delivery bicycle.

THE MIDLAND HOTEL which stood adjacent to West Station. By August 1884 it is recorded that over 6,000 visitors a day were arriving at the station, many of whom must have stayed at the Midland which was 'replete with every accommodation'. It had 'electric light, and telephonic communication with all parts of Bournemouth'. It is shown here in 1901.

POOLE HILL C. 1905. The round building at the bottom left of Poole Hill is Pars and Co., Bournemouth's oldest pharmacy, which closed in 1979 after 103 years. The Regency fittings came from a chemist's shop in London, and the shop was built in a circular shape to house them. Further down on the right is Orchard Street, Bournemouth's only 'street'.

MUSSELWHITE AND SIMPKINS, cabinet makers, at their works in Avenue Lane, c. 1901.

COUNTY GATES, BOURNEMOUTH.

COUNTY GATES in 1900. The vehicle on the right is a mystery. Can anyone identify it?

A LONE HORSE CARRIAGE proceeds along The Avenue in around 1905.

SECTION SIX

Boscombe

A PARLEY ON BOSCOMBE HILL in 1862, presenting an almost unrecognizable scene. On the left is the future site of the Linden Hall Hydro and, on the right, the site of Boscombe Gardens.

CHRISTCHURCH ROAD, BOSCOMBE, in 1876, when it was evidently little more than a country road. At this time Boscombe consisted merely of a few scattered mud-wall cottages and this wayside inn, the Ragged Cat, later the Palmerston Arms.

SEA ROAD, Boscombe, 1870. This area today is a mass of houses.

BOSCOMBE PIER, pictured here in around 1902, was built in 1888, the first pile having been driven by Lady Shelley. The solitary figure on the left stands in marked contrast to the thousands that throng the sea front today.

THE MARINA, pictured in around 1900. Formerly known as Bascombe, it appears on maps long before the existence of Bournemouth and in 1838 was referred to as 'a dwelling in the wilderness'. The Chine Gardens were laid out on the site of an earlier brick kiln.

THE POLICEMAN outside the Arcade seems to have had time on his hands when this picture, looking along Christchurch Road, was taken in 1901. The Arcade then contained 30 'handsome and commodious shops', and concerts were given daily. Written in stone above the Arcade are the words 'Music Daily', and 'Band and Organ'.

THE CAMERA NEVER LIES. Aeroplanes were first seen over Bournemouth in 1910 during the Bournemouth Aviation Meeting. One would imagine that this sight would have stopped the traffic, yet this aeroplane seems to have met with a definite lack of interest. It was in fact never there, having been drawn in by an artist at some later date!

ONLY FIVE YEARS separate this 1906 view from the one above.

BOSCOMBE SANDS at the close of the last century. There are a few rowing boats for hire, bathing machines stand at the water's edge and Bournemouth pier is visible in the distance.

A BUSY SCENE at the turn of the century, when the thing to do was to stand fully clothed at the water's edge. A parasol kept the sun off but not the heat. These holidaymakers must have absolutely baked!

2 BOSCOMBE. — *View from the Pier.* — LL.

BATH CHAIRS AND DECKCHAIRS. This was the prospect from the pier in around 1903.

BOSCOMBE PIER in 1900. Officially opened in 1889 by the Duke of Argyll, it was never successful and soon was bought by Bournemouth Corporation, which introduced roller-skating and held a grand reopening in 1904.

Boscombe from Pier

THE PIER IN ITS PRIME in around 1910.

RUSTIC BRIDGE, THE GARDENS.   BOSCOMBE.

Dear Mrs Neevil. I thought you would like this view, because there is such a lovely walk for lovers if you take you a turning on the left such a leafy spot, do you think my something is improving a little, I am trying for your sake it is not my fault. That is all on these pens or ale a back love Banks

A LOVELY WALK FOR LOVERS – such a leafy spot. The Rustic Bridge in the days when you could send a postcard locally to say you were coming to tea that afternoon!

THE UNDERCLIFF DRIVE, BOSCOMBE

'BOSCOMBE SPA' grew up around a mineral spring which, it was said, had similar qualities to Harrogate Water. Boscombe was later to become associated with the Shelley family, who lived at Boscombe Manor.

The Band Stand Christchurch Road, Boscombe.

A CONCERT IN THE BANDSTAND in Boscombe Crescent Gardens.

BOSCOMBE HILL, May 1908. A tram struggles past the later site of the Linden Hall.

THE LINDEN HALL, which was demolished in 1986.

SECTION SEVEN

Winton

Winton, Bournemouth.

TRAVELLERS passing this way during the 1880s sometimes complained of having 'sods and brickbats' thrown at them by the 'wild and fierce' inhabitants. However true, Winton at the turn of the century was a 'rapidly growing artisan district', becoming part of Bournemouth in 1901. It is shown here c. 1906.

MARK LOADER'S GANG pose on the first tree cut in the making of Bryanstone Road in 1900. St Luke's Church, built only two years previously, can be seen in the background.

THE SAME VIEW of Bryanstone Road in 1968, showing St Luke's Church.

TALBOT PARADE in around 1906. The newspaper shop on the corner of Bryanstone Road became the National Westminster Bank, and today's Barclays on the opposite corner was not yet in existence. St Luke's Road is not yet cut through, nor has Alma Road yet extended into Wimborne Road. Note the distinctive turrets on the Boots building for a comparison with the photograph below.

THE BANKS, with the Plaza Cinema, later the Continental, on the right. There is, of course, no High Street in Winton. This is Wimborne Road.

WIMBORNE ROAD, C. 1906. Bailey's, on the left, used to be a cycle shop and outside hung a giant bicycle wheel. It was later to become Bailey's Hairdressers, and the wheel was covered over with something – but does anyone know what?

THE PREMISES OF STURTON'S FURNISHING STORES in around 1907. Mr Sturton stands second from the left with the staff at the entrance to his store.

THE CORNER OF PRIVET ROAD. On the right is the premises of Ashley Mews, makers of charabancs, brakes, and 'open and close' carriages. Mr Dowding is outside, leaning on his stick.

THE SAME VIEW as above a few years later, showing Bellamy's on the left and Bailey's further down on the right.

TROKE'S – BAKER'S, GROCER'S, AND SUB-POST OFFICE in Wimborne Road in 1870, when travellers from Winton would have crossed rough land to reach Bournemouth. Is that Mr Troke in his postmaster's uniform?

TROKE'S in 1902. A magnifying glass reveals that here Colman's Starch, Sunlight Soap, Bird's Custard and assorted products from Rowntree's and Peek Freens were sold, in the days when goods were not 'displayed' but literally crammed into the windows.

PREMISES OF COLES, coal merchant, in 1902, when the coal waggons line up for the camera.

COLES had become a butcher's shop by 1906.

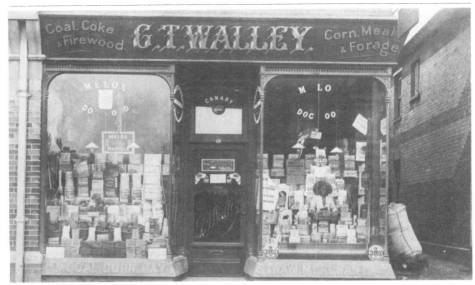

G.T. WALLEY'S C. 1908. Prices used to be painted on windows, and it looks as if these first experiments in 'stick-on' letters were not always successful.

NOS. 408–414 WIMBORNE ROAD in around 1905, showing G.T. Walley's on the right.

CINEMA-GOERS AT THE PLAZA, later the Continental.

SHERRY THE BAKER of Wimborne Road, showing Mr Sherry with his assistant in the
doorway of his shop, c. 1895.

WIMBORNE ROAD, Moordown, with Swan's newspaper shop at the corner of Queen Mary Avenue on the right. Elmer Road is on the left.

MOORDOWN was little more than a hamlet at the close of the century. It is pictured here, in around 1905, with Phillips the chemists at the corner of King George Avenue to the right, and Renie's Ladies Shop on the far corner of Cowper Road to the left.

Around Bournemouth

TRAMS AT CEMETERY GATES. Bournemouth bought a number of its trams from Cheltenham. On the left, is tramcar No. 21, a Cheltenham English Electric Car which served in Bournemouth between 1921 and 1930. For the next 30 years it was used as a store in a market garden near Cheltenham, but today is housed in the Bournemouth Transport Museum.

CLIFF COTTAGE, where Charles Darwin, already famous for his *Origin of Species*, stayed in 1862. The cottage was situated on the West Cliff on a site just east of the Highcliff Hotel, near the old coastguard station. Its name is perpetuated today by Cliff Cottage Road.

THE PINE WALK on the West Cliff.

THE SCENE AT CEMETERY GATES in around 1901. Built in 1878, its avenues were lined with auricarias.

JACK LOVE, taxi driver of Cardigan Road, Winton, sits with his wife on the first tree felled during the making of Glenferness Avenue in 1912.

THE LANSDOWNE in 1870, taken from Bath Road. At the junction of Holdenhurst and Christchurch Roads stands Lansdown House, later to be the site of the Hotel Metropole and the Royal London House. The road was then not properly made up: there was no drainage and consequently no gutters.

LOOKING DOWN OLD CHRISTCHURCH ROAD in 1868, viewed from a point on Horseshoe Common. St Peter's stands towerless on the left.

F.47005. BOURNEMOUTH: MUNICIPAL COLLEGE.

THE MUNICIPAL COLLEGE AND PUBLIC LIBRARY were opened in 1913, and are pictured here shortly after that date. A tram proceeds along Christchurch Road, a taxi stands outside the Hotel Metropole on the left and taxi carriages wait for hire along the Bath Road.

HORSE-DRAWN REMOVALS *c.* 1900. White and Co.'s two-horse pantechnicon.

THE IMPERIAL HOTEL, which was at the Lansdowne opposite the Metropole, pictured in 1908. It was later to become the site of the Round House and Crest Hotels.

THE QUEEN HOTEL, at the junction of Bath Road and Old Christchurch Road, in 1921.

HOLDENHURST ROAD c. 1905. Tramcar No. 35, *en route* to Boscombe, passes the fire station on the right, and a cyclist, on the left, appears to be clutching two new wheels for his bicycle.

THE SOUTH WESTERN HOTEL, in Holdenhurst Road opposite the Central Station, in 1921.

HORSESHOE COMMON in 1901. On the corner of Dean Park Road are W.C. Hooker's, and Slade and Wood's music stores, while on the right can be seen the gorse and pines which originally covered the area.

THE VIEW FROM ST PETER'S SPIRE in 1877, showing the fine detached villas in Westover Road and Hinton Road. In the distance is the old wooden pier in its damaged condition after a great gale in the previous year had shortened it by 1,000 ft. Wreckage was found as far away as Swanage.

A SOLITARY FIGURE climbs Old Christchurch Road in 1878, photographed from the tower of Holy Trinity, which had been completed the same year.

BARROWS at the junction of Southcote and St Swithun's Road in 1921.

ST SWITHUN'S ROAD, showing the premises of G.R. Melmoth, undertaker.

TOWER HOUSE, No. 2 Southcote Road. Outside, the barrowmen enjoy a leisurely smoke.

WAVERLEY ROAD, with the printing works on the right. All the photographs on these two pages were taken in 1921.

KNYVETON ROAD in 1921, and not a car in sight!

FRANCES ROAD, also pictured in 1921.

AN ENTRANCE TO THE TALBOT WOODS, c. 1905. Situated about half-way between what is now Stirling Road and Talbot Avenue, this lodge stood at the head of the principal drive through the 'Bournemouth Pines'. Mr Fred Cannon, an old resident of Winton and a Bournemouth butcher, recalls how he would race from school to the gates in order to earn a copper or two by opening them for the local gentry passing through in their carriages on their way to Westbourne. Below, the same spot in 1963.

WALLISDOWN CROSSROADS in 1913, today a very busy junction. Below, the same location in 1963.

MEYRICK PARK GOLF LINKS showing the Pavilion at the top of the rise. At the turn of the century there were ladies' and gentlemen's Links here, the former having nine holes and the latter eighteen.

The Golf-Links, Bournemouth.

A VIEW OVER BOURNEMOUTH and the Golf Links in around 1902.

THE ENCLOSURES AND STRAIGHT at Bournemouth Racecourse in 1925.

THE RACECOURSE, showing the grandstand in Ensbury Park.

CHARMINSTER ROAD c. 1905. The posts on the left carry the overhead tramwires. On the right is H.W. King's, cycle makers and greengrocers and beyond the china and glass shop is Pearce's Circulating Library.

SLADE AND WOOD'S music stores, Horseshoe Common, in around 1901. Pianos, one standing in each window, were offered for sale or hire, or one could take advantage of their 'Circulating Musical Library'.

CAN ANYONE RECALL any of these visitors to Bournemouth? Perhaps someone might recognize the monocled lady on the right or the smiling gentleman on the left with the cigarette. Is that his wife and daughter beside him?

THE GRAND HOTEL, Fir Vale Road, in 1921. Originally known as the Grand Fir Vale Hotel, it was, in its prime, a magnificent and luxurious hotel that once covered three acres. This view was taken from the rear.

IN THE LAST CENTURY Pokesdown presented a rural and tranquil scene. It was then a small village on the road to Christchurch, with a few scattered mud-wall cottages.

PARKWOOD ROAD, Pokesdown. This area was originally known at Puck's Down.

TWO VIEWS OF IFORD BRIDGE in around 1901. Iford was then a picturesque village of thatched and white-walled cottages standing along dusty, unmade roads. In 1851 a sturgeon was caught in the Stour here that weighed 109 lb, and measured over 7 ft long.

THE WATERWORKS at Tuckton where followers of Tolstoy set up a printing press. The waterworks were built in 1875 to pump water from the Stour up to Southbourne Water Tower. It was sold shortly after and leased to Count Vladimir Chertkov, who set up the Free Age Press, printing Tolstoy's political ideas which were considered subversive in Russia. The Press was disbanded in 1908 and the building sold to the Kiddles, who latterly used it as a car respray business. These buildings have now been converted into residential houses.

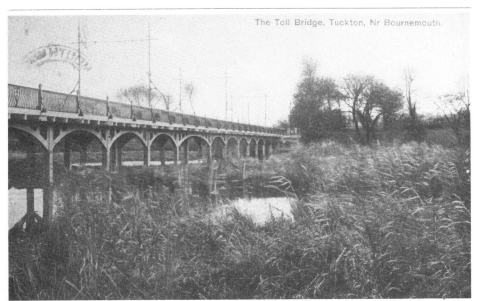

TUCKTON TOLL-BRIDGE c. 1906. The original bridge of 1822 was completely rebuilt and reopened in 1905. The toll was 6d. for four-wheeled vehicles, 4d. for two-wheeled vehicles, passengers in vehicles 1d., bicycles and perambulators paying $\frac{1}{2}d$.

STOURWOOD ROAD, SOUTHBOURNE. Dr Compton, a Bournemouth physician, had bought land here in 1870, visualizing a resort that would rival Bournemouth but, in 1880, Southbourne still had neither name nor road, much less a house. Stourwood Road is shown here in around 1900, when the neighbourhood was said to 'abound in interesting walks and drives'.

FISHERMAN'S WALK. Local fishermen would use this path on their way to the cliffs to watch for incoming shoals of mackerel.

THE CLIFFS AT FISHERMANS WALK.

SOUTHBOURNE PIER in 1894. The pier was damaged time and again by stormy seas and was soon entirely destroyed. After remaining derelict for several years it was eventually demolished. Southbourne originally had an Undercliff Esplanade, but this too became broken up by the sea. The whole area is today under water.

The Wrecked Pier, Southbourne

The Chines

THE SUSPENSION BRIDGE, Alum Chine, built shortly after the completion of the Undercliff Drive in 1902.

THE RUSTIC BRIDGE, Alum Chine. The dictionary defines a chine as 'a deep, narrow ravine' but Winston Churchill was more eloquent when he said that Alum Chine is 'a small, wild place, where forty or fifty acres of pine forest descend by sandy undulations to the smooth beach of the English Channel'.

A PEEP IN ALUM CHINE, in around 1911, showing St Ambrose Church.

SIR WINSTON CHURCHILL nearly lost his life in a reckless escapade on this rustic bridge, seen here in around 1900. In 1893, soon after his eighteenth birthday, he was on holiday at nearby Branksome Dene, the home of his aunt, Lady Wimborne. During a game of chase he found himself trapped on the bridge with his younger brother, aged 12, and a cousin, aged 14, at either end. The Chine was then full of slender fir trees and Sir Winston later wrote 'Would it not, I asked myself, be possible to leap onto one of them and slip down the pole-like stem, breaking off each tier of branches as one descended until the fall was broken?' But unfortunately, 'the argument was correct; the data absolutely wrong'. He plunged almost 30 ft onto hard ground and, among other injuries, ruptured a kidney and was in a coma for three days. It was two months before he had recovered sufficiently to resume his studies in London.

ALUM, used in the tanning trade, was mined here in the sixteenth century, but the venture was short lived and unsuccessful, causing the ruin of the Lord of the Manor at Canford, who was behind the scheme. The suspension bridge replaced the earlier rustic bridge, and is shown here in around 1909.

SKERRYVORE, The home of Robert Louis Stevenson between 1885 and 1887. Here, despite serious ill-health, he wrote *Kidnapped* and *Dr Jekyll and Mr Hyde* and, according to his own description, lived here 'like a weevil in a biscuit'. Skerryvore, which stood at the head of Alum Chine, was severely damaged by a land mine in 1940 and was later demolished. It is now a memorial garden.

BRANKSOME CHINE c. 1901, showing the lake. The chine was a favourite landing place for smugglers such as 'Slippery Rogers' and particularly the celebrated 'Old Gulliver'.

THE SAME VIEW around 15 years earlier, in the late 1880s, photographed by Mr G.W. Taylor, the Westbourne chemist.

BRANKSOME CHINE in around 1901. The Chines were the haunt of the notorious Neville Heath whose second victim, Doreen Marshall, was found in 1946 horribly murdered under a rhododendron bush in the nearby Branksome Dene Chine.

THE SEA FRONT at Branksome Chine in the early 1950s. In the car park is a car collector's delight; a magnifying glass reveals a Bentley Drophead, a Railton, a Standard 8 and a Standard Flying 8, a Morris E Type, a Rover 12, an Austin Devon, etc.

THE MINIATURE ENGLISH CHANNEL at Branksome Chine. As a boy the author used to enjoy jumping from Bournemouth to the Isle of Wight!

DURLEY CHINE marked the border with Dorset until 1818 when it was moved to Alum Chine. In 1974 Bournemouth became part of Dorset.

WHITE CLAY was found at Durley Chine in the early nineteenth century and was sent to the potteries in Staffordshire as the purest and best material for the celebrated porcelains of the district.

BOSCOMBE CHINE GARDENS at the turn of the century. This area was once a pine wood.

SECTION TEN

Events

AUGUST BANK HOLIDAY, 1890. An amusement fair on the east beach.

THE GREAT TRAM ACCIDENT of 1 May 1908 was at the time 'the most shocking disaster that has ever occurred in the history of Bournemouth', and was the country's first and largest tram accident. Tramcar No. 72, *en route* from Poole to Southbourne with around 30 passengers on board, approached the Square at its normal speed of about 8 m.p.h. when the brakes failed. Careering down Avenue Road at nearly 75 m.p.h., it failed to negotiate the bend and plunged into Fairlight Glen, part of the Upper Gardens behind today's Marks and Spencers. Seven died and twenty-six were injured. William Walton, the driver, became one of Bournemouth's first heroes when, although badly injured, he fought to save lives before he collapsed himself. He was cleared of all blame and went on to become an inspector.

TRAMCAR NO. 72 was repaired and renumbered No. 71, and continued in service until 1935. It later became living accommodation for Charlie and Bernie Bishop, who lived in it near Lychett Matravers with their two children until 1977. Unaware of its grisly past, they say it made excellent living accommodation.

THE BOURNEMOUTH CENTENARY FÊTES took place in July 1910. Some of the floats came from Italy; this particular example was called 'Cock of the Day'.

THE ARREST OF THE ROGUES. Part of the Centenary Fêtes in Meyrick Park.

THE SQUARE BEDECKED WITH BUNTING. Carnivals, confetti battles and a motor cavalcade were all part of the celebrations. Suffragettes took advantage of the fêtes to press their demands for votes for women.

THE CENTENARY CAR.

TUCKTON BRIDGE was rebuilt and is pictured here at its reopening on 17 October 1905. It had been a toll-bridge since its construction in 1822.

THE HON. CHARLES STUART ROLLS, of Rolls Royce fame, died moments after this picture was taken at about 1 p.m. on 12 July 1910. He was flying this Short Wright biplane in the International Aviation Meeting in Southbourne, and was attempting to land on the spot when the tail snapped off and the machine broke up. It was the first fatal flying accident in this country.

THE TRAM-O-CAR'S DISASTROUS PLUNGE, 20 July 1932. From the *Times and Directory*: 'Wednesday's tragic occurrence at Boscombe Pier, where a corporation tram-o-car crashed through the esplanade railings onto the beach below, killing two women on the sands and injuring others. The vehicle, temporarily unattended, started to move of its own accord from near the entrance to the Overstrand Cafe, and though the driver tried to board it he was unable to check its plunge onto the beach.'

TEN GERMAN FIGHTER BOMBERS swooped low over the roof-tops of Bournemouth on 23 May 1943, at 1 p.m., dropping bombs on the town centre and other residential districts. Bournemouth's most extensive air raid of the war occurred at a Sunday lunchtime and fortunately the streets were fairly empty, but casualties were nevertheless heavy. Pictured above is the Central Hotel at the foot of Richmond Hill which received a direct hit, wrecking the adjacent Punshon Memorial Church in the blast. A policeman on duty was shot at, ('I don't know how they missed me', he said) and a young man sitting on a bench with a girl was severely wounded by machine gun bullets. Trapped in the wreckage of the hotel was Mrs Badcock of Newton Abbot, who chatted cheerfully to rescuers and directed operations during the $19\frac{1}{2}$ hours it took to extricate her.

BEALES DEPARTMENT STORE received a direct hit and was completely gutted in the fire that raged all afternoon. Below, the magnificent clock with moving figures which hung outside the art deco building lies shattered among the rubble.

THE HOTEL METROPOLE, which was bombed just at the time many RAF and Canadian troops had sat down to lunch. Many people were trapped in the ruins including a bus conductor complete with work bag and bicycle. In all, nearly 3,500 buildings were damaged and 77 people died.

THREE ENEMY PLANES were downed and this Focke Wulf 190 was claimed by an RAF pilot as his first kill.

SECTION ELEVEN

Transport

BOURNEMOUTH CENTRAL c. 1905. This view shows how the ladies' rooms were divided into first, second and third classes. In 1910 the Pullman Express took two hours ten minutes to Waterloo.

THE CENTRAL STATION, opened in 1885 replaced the first station of 1870, which was situated in what is now the goods yard. Bournemouth West and East were not linked until 1888.

A STEAM RAILCAR at the 'up' platform just after the turn of the century. The station was known as Bournemouth East until it was renamed Bournemouth Central in 1899.

IN THE DAYS OF STEAM, when this picture was taken c. 1903, a second class return to Waterloo cost 19s. 9d.

AN EARLY VIEW of Boscombe Station.

BOURNEMOUTH WEST STATION in 1901. This tranquil scene belies the fact that, as early as August 1884, 6,500 trippers had arrived on one day alone. Bournemouth's second station had direct connections with the Midlands and West Country. It closed in 1965.

POKESDOWN STATION, under construction here, was opened in 1886.

TRAMCAR NO. 108 in Boscombe, *en route* to Christchurch. Bournemouth trams had upstairs seats which had double sides; if wet, one could flip the slatted seat over to the dry side. The back rest was hinged so that it could face either direction. Inside, the saloon had wooden fittings, stained glass panels along the roof, and 'No Spitting' notices, for fear of tuberculosis.

A TILLING STEVENS petrol electric bus of 1914.

TROLLEY BUSSES replaced the trams in 1936. This unusual picture shows both in service –
presumably in 1936.

SECTION TWELVE

Music and Entertainment

DAN GODFREY, champion of British music, with the Municipal Orchestra in the old Winter Gardens in around 1900. The band are surrounded by tiers of potted plants appearing, according to *Punch*, as if 'planted among the ferns'.

THE ITALIAN BAND, 1893. The original band numbered 16 musicians and had come to Bournemouth in 1876 following an engagement in Bath, intending to stay for only one season, but they were retained by public subscription. As ex-members of the Italian army, they were entitled to wear military uniform, and played military style music on the pier and in the Gardens. From these beginnings the Bournemouth Symphony Orchestra grew.

THE OLD WINTER GARDENS in around 1905. It was built in 1876 when glass pavilions in the style of the Crystal Palace were very much the vogue. The fairy lights, with candles in coloured glass pots, are still a feature of Bournemouth.

ORCHESTRAL CONCERTS IN THE WINTER GARDENS were popularized by Dan Godfrey. On the day of the first concerts in May 1933, 10,000 people paid the 3d. admission to the grounds.

THE MUNICIPAL CHOIR was formed in 1911, although choral works had been performed as early as 1897, when the programme included Parry's 'Ode To St Cecilia's Day'.

DAN GODFREY (seated) was appointed musical director in 1893, a post he held for 41 years. At this time the band was divided into two, providing a string section for the Winter Gardens and a military band for the pier. Pictured here are the motley crew on their annual outing in 1895. Spot the large hat, and the superbly cocky stance of the bandsman on the right.

BILLY BYRNE, 'Old Bill' to his friends, the timpanist who became a legend.

BRITISH COMPOSERS frequently conducted their own music at the Winter Gardens. Pictured here in 1910 for a special concert are, from left to right: Sir Edward Elgar, Sir Edward German, Dan Godfrey, Sir Alexander Mackenzie, Sir Hubert Parry and Sir Charles Stanford.

THE MUNICIPAL ORCHESTRA in 1926. Dan Godfrey was knighted in 1922 and became a household name when the concerts were regularly broadcast in the 1920s and '30s. The orchestra moved to the new Pavilion in 1929.

THE GLASS HOUSE, the old greenhouse, the hothouse, the kitchen garden, the cucumber frame, the conservatory: members of the orchestra used to vie with one another to find rude names for the Winter Gardens. Its unpopularity with the orchestra was perhaps justified; pianissimo passages were ruined during inclement weather by the roar of rain on the roof. With such puddles visible on the floor, one hopes that they were able to keep their instruments dry!

THE WINTER GARDENS in 1893. At this time the orchestra numbered 25 members. The pine woods situated here were once the favourite spot of Louis Tregonwell, founder of Bournemouth, who named them Cranborne Gardens.

OPEN AIR CONCERTS were a popular feature when this picture was taken in around 1903. The Bournemouth orchestra was the country's first permanent municipal orchestra and became the Bournemouth Symphony Orchestra in 1954.

FAMOUS NAMES at the Winter Gardens during a festival of 1922 in which all shared the conducting. From the left, Sir Alexander Mackenzie, Dame Ethel Smyth, Dan Godfrey, Sir Henry Wood and Sir Edward German.

SIR JOHN BARBIROLLI, who conducted here during the festival of 1951.

CONSTANTIN SILVESTRI, conductor from 1961, took the orchestra across Europe to ecstatic reviews. He died in 1969 and was buried in St Peter's churchyard.

THE ORCHESTRA under Rudolf Schwarz in 1950.

THE PAVILION, intended as a new home for the Municipal Orchestra, was built on the site of the old Belle Vue Hotel and opened in 1929.

THE BOURNEMOUTH BATHS, home of the 'Aquashows' in later years. The first baths on this site were built in the late 1850s.

PERCY WHITLOCK at the console of the Pavilion's Compton Organ in June 1932. Mr Whitlock came to Bournemouth as organist of St Stephens, but soon moved to the Pavilion. An accomplished organist and composer, he gave many broadcasts from the Pavilion and around the country. With an interest in clocks and mechanical things his home was a treasure trove of the unusual. He even had built a pedal pipe organ with the console in one room, the pipework in the basement, more pipes in the chimneys, and the blower in what had been the coal shed!

THE WESTOVER ICE RINK in the 1930s.

THE WORLD'S FIRST ICE SHOW was presented at the Ice Rink in 1931, produced by John Neal, manager and later managing director. Pictured here is the cast of *Gay Vienna* in 1934 which starred Phil Taylor, Erna Charlotte and Baron Von Petersdorf (middle group). Apart from during the war years, Mr Neal produced and made many of the props for these spectacular shows until 1980.

LARS GRAFSTRÖM, the Swedish skater, in the 1930s, giving a display on a block of ice containing flowers – another prop made by John Neal.

PREPARING FOR THE WALTZ, c. 1932.

'ALL SKATE'. The old milk bar is in the background on the left and at the front is Barbara Matthews, a skating star in later years.

THE BOURNEMOUTH DOMINOES.